A Song for Every Morning

Dedication and Defiance with St Patrick's Breastplate

John Davies

CANTERBURY
PRESS
Norwich

© John Davies 2008

First published in 2008 by the Canterbury Press Norwich
(a publishing imprint of Hymns Ancient & Modern Limited,
a registered charity)
13–17 Long Lane, London EC1A 9PN

www.scm-canterburypress.co.uk

British Library Cataloguing in Publication data

A catalogue record for this book is available
from the British Library

ISBN 978-1-85311-847-0

Typeset by Regent Typesetting, London
Printed and bound by
Biddles Ltd, King's Lynn, Norfolk

Contents

Foreword

On being asked what in the life of the Iona Community he would defend to his last breath, one member thought for a moment then said, 'St Patrick's Breastplate in the Hallowing Service.' And indeed, though they might not express it so vehemently, I think that the vast majority of members would agree that the singing of it in our annual service of rededication to our commitment and the confirmation of new members into full members holds a special and unique place in our affections. We sing it in the six-verse version of Mrs Cecil Frances Alexander to the Irish traditional tune 'St Patrick', and it has many resonances for us as a community. It reminds us of the Celtic traditions and inheritance of St Columba or Columkille, the apostle of Iona and bringer of Christianity to Scotland, who we remember every day in our Community prayers. It allows us to do together wholeheartedly something that binds us as a community, that is, to sing. And it reiterates themes of faith which are of great importance to us in our own life and work.

The various themes of the Breastplate – the themes of protection and encompassing; of the Trinitarian nature of our faith (as John Davies says, we understand the Trinity not as a problem but a blessing), which connects us back not just to the Celtic saints but to their antecedents in St Martin of Tours, the Desert Fathers, and the riches of the Orthodox tradition, and binds us to the unity of God and the community of God; of the Incarnation, Emmanuel, God-with-us; of reverence and respect for God in creation and our place within the natural order; of judgement and personal responsibility; of Christ our guide and our end – all these themes find expression in the work and worship of the present-day Iona Community. More than that, we wish to be marked by them, for they are central to our self-understanding. For members of the Iona Community, this book will be an invaluable insight and guide into what for us is more than just one of the great hymns of the Christian church, but is almost a statement of faith.

The value of this book goes well beyond the Iona Community, however, and beyond those with an interest in Celtic Christianity. These are themes that touch the hearts of all Christians, and that will help them to reflect, pray and act in the spirit of the gospel to which John Davies points us in a contemporary context, just as the hymn does for an earlier time. It is a song of praise to sing, an affirmation of faith to step out on, a prayer of lively hope and trust in protection and guidance that brings the personal and the political, the spiritual and the material together in a celebration of the God who is both Three and One. Singing the song will be enhanced by reading this book.

Kathy Galloway
Leader, Iona Community

Acknowledgements

The design on page 9 is adapted from a pattern included in *The Triads of Britain*, by William MacLellan and Bill Butler (London, Wildwood House, 1977, p. 12).

The direct translation of the original Irish of 'St Patrick's Breastplate' at the end of this book is taken from *The Primal Vision*, by John V. Taylor (London, SCM Press, 1963, pp. 204f.)

This book has been developed from articles contributed to the *Church Times* in 2004; some of these were edited for inclusion in *The Church Times Book of 100 Best Prayers* (London, SCM-Canterbury Press, 2006). The author is grateful to the *Church Times* for agreeing to this use of the material.

Introduction

Patrick's song – my story

'St Patrick's Breastplate' caught me just when it was needed, on the night before my ordination as a priest over 50 years ago. For several weeks, while I was still a deacon, I had been feeling that the whole idea of Christian ministry was not for me, and I was thinking of packing it in. The Breastplate helped to form my new commitment, and it has been my first morning prayer ever since. We sang it (though, sadly, not all nine verses!) when I was consecrated bishop.

Fifty years ago, I had never heard of Celtic spirituality. The Breastplate affirms the central truths of God as Trinity and of Christ's incarnation; it affirms God's presence in this world of creation. These are the outstanding themes of Celtic Christian spirituality, according to the scholars of our tribes. Whether Celtic or not, to me this is orthodox Christian faith. But then perhaps, as a Welshman, I'm biased.

This book consists of some personal reflections on the verses that are nowadays commonly called 'St Patrick's Breastplate'. This prayer, in its original form, probably dates from about 300 years later than St Patrick himself. The 'Breastplate' was a favourite form of prayer and commitment among Celtic Christians, and this is the best-known example; it has always been linked with the name of Patrick, who had to stand for the truth of God amid the cruelty and tyranny of his day. We supply a direct translation of the original text at the end of the book. This is in the form that John Vernon Taylor (later Bishop of Winchester) quoted at the conclusion of his *The Primal Vision* (SCM Press, 1963), a book that was of great value in the 1960s as a window for Europeans into the insights and struggles of African spirituality. As he says, the Celtic spirituality of the Breastplate flows directly from the witness of the New Testament Letters to the Ephesians and Colossians; it can provide a bridge between Africa's awareness of the divine presence in creation and the heartlands of Christian teaching: 'It sums up and contains all the spiritual awareness of the primal vision and lifts it into the fullness of Christ. Would that it were translated and sung in every tongue of Africa!' So it will not only be the devotees of the Celtic traditions who will recognize the power of this text, but also all who resonate with the spiritual yearnings of Africa.

I do not offer this book as a scholarly analysis, but as

a personal testimony. For this reason I base it not on the original text, but on the version that was made popular in the hymn books of the earlier years of the twentieth century. This is the version that first caught my attention and has held it ever since. We owe it to Cecil Frances Alexander, of Northern Ireland. If we compare it with the original, we see that Mrs Alexander has not merely translated the original into English; she has developed it into a considerably extended poem. She has also made it more accessible and memorable by putting it into regular verses. As in her other popular hymns, her language is remarkably free of 'thous' and 'wasts', so it needs little modernization for use today. Her version has been made even more memorable by the magnificent old Irish melodies with which it has been associated, through the skill of another Irish colleague, the musical editor Charles Villiers Stanford.

So I take the text of the Breastplate from *The English Hymnal* and *Hymns Ancient And Modern*. Later in the book I will observe that even the more traditional of the newer hymn books omit large sections of the Breastplate. This is happening at a time when, in my view, the message of these omitted verses could be of great value in the spiritual struggle for the blessedness of God's creation and against the corruption of that creation by the powers of evil. A 'breastplate' is, after all, essentially equipment for defence. So, I offer this book as a small attempt to reinstate the whole Breastplate as a prayer and as a resource for our discipleship.

I am especially grateful to Kathy Galloway, Leader of the Iona Community, for her perceptive Foreword to this book. The Community is well known for its creativity in song and liturgy, but this attractive image is not a thing in itself. It is generated by the Community's wider commitment to justice and peace, to the struggle against policies of dependence on nuclear weaponry, to the honouring of all members of the human family irrespective of their race or sexuality, to the recognition of God's claim upon the earth and the material world and, over all, to the celebration of new life and hope in Jesus Christ. Because of the vigour of these commitments, the Community has attracted my wife Shirley and myself into Associate Membership for many years. And these commitments resonate with the spirituality of dedication and defiance that flourish at every verse of St Patrick's Breastplate.

John D. Davies
Gobowen
Festival of St David/Gŵyl Ddewi 2007

'St Patrick's Breastplate': the popular hymn version

The version of 'St Patrick's Breastplate' used in this book is the adaptation by Mrs Cecil Frances Alexander, which has been popular as a hymn from the early twentieth century.

> I bind unto myself today
> The strong name of the Trinity,
> By invocation of the same,
> The Three in One and One in Three.
>
> I bind this today to me for ever,
> By power of faith, Christ's Incarnation;
> His baptism in Jordan river;
> His death on Cross for my salvation;
> His bursting from the spiced tomb;
> His riding up the heavenly way;
> His coming at the day of doom;
> I bind unto myself today.

I bind unto myself the power
Of the great love of Cherubim;
The sweet 'Well done' in judgement hour;
The service of the Seraphim,
Confessors' faith, Apostles' word,
The Patriarchs' prayers, the Prophets' scrolls,
All good deeds done unto the Lord,
And purity of virgin souls.

I bind unto myself today
The virtues of the starlit heaven,
The glorious sun's life-giving ray,
The whiteness of the moon at even,
The flashing of the lightning free,
The whirling wind's tempestuous shocks,
The stable earth, the deep salt sea,
Around the old eternal rocks.

I bind unto myself today
The power of God to hold and lead,
His eye to watch, His might to stay,
His ear to hearken to my need.
The wisdom of my God to teach,
His hand to guide, His shield to ward;
The word of God to give me speech,
His heavenly host to be my guard.

Against the demon snares of sin,
The vice that gives temptation force,
The natural lusts that war within,
The hostile men that mar my course;
Or few or many, far or nigh,
In every place and in all hours,
Against their fierce hostility,
I bind to me these holy powers.

Against all Satan's spells and wiles,
Against false words of heresy,
Against the knowledge that defiles,
Against the heart's idolatry,
Against the wizard's evil craft,
Against the death-wound and the burning,
The choking wave, the poisoned shaft,
Protect me, Christ, till thy returning.

Christ be with me, Christ within me,
Christ behind me, Christ before me,
Christ beside me, Christ to win me,
Christ to comfort and restore me,
Christ beneath me, Christ above me,
Christ in quiet, Christ in danger,
Christ in hearts of all that love me,
Christ in mouth of friend and stranger.

I bind unto myself the name,
The strong name of the Trinity;
By invocation of the same,
The Three in One and One in Three.
Of whom all nature hath creation;
Eternal Father, Spirit, Word:
Praise to the Lord of my salvation,
Salvation is of Christ the Lord.

I Bind unto Myself Today

I bind unto myself today

'I bind to myself'. The verses reflected upon in this book are a prayer in the traditional Breastplate form. They recite the clothing that the Christian pilgrim puts on at the beginning of the day, just as we lace up our shoes or button up our coats. This idea goes back to Chapter 6 of the Letter to the Ephesians. In his prison cell, the apostle Paul is able to observe all the military equipment of the guard who is keeping him captive. Paul is freer than his guards; all they can do is to imprison their victim. The apostle is free to think and sing and pray; with this freedom, he is able to check through the instruments of death and domination, the items of uniform representing an empire of oppression and violence, the insignia of a system that had crucified the Son of God.

He is able to reinvent them as images of God's equipment, the trousers of truth, the shirt of justice, the boots of peace, and so on. God provides the Breastplate, just as the Ministry of Defence equips its personnel. As an Airframe Fitter in the Royal Air Force, I was provided with equipment for the work, a box of spanners and gauges; and they certainly weren't given to me as subjects for philosophical discussions, or for making pretty patterns on the hangar wall. In the same way, we are expected to use the Breastplate, and to keep it in good order.

So, at the beginning of the day, I claim the Breastplate as my protection, as my identity. With this defence, I can defy the assumptions and priorities that will come at me during the day, from outside myself and from within. I was most consciously claiming this defence during the 14 years when I was in South Africa. We were a community of Christians who were trying to work out our commitment and obedience amid the heresies and cruelties of apartheid. But the basic claims remain valid, wherever we are.

The Breastplate is a morning song, a greeting for the new day. The new day is never just a repetition of yesterday. It will have its own particular opportunities, dangers and possibilities. Even if

I am apparently stuck, trapped by disability or immobilized by anxiety, it is a new day. There will be fresh items on the news to engage my prayer, and the words will fit in a different way that is both universal and particular. And the day will be one more step towards my own death. So the words will not become mere repetition. But I would expect that on any particular day, some verses will have more immediate relevance than others. Further, in the solidarity of the community of faith, there will be people for whom we can make the affirmation of the Breastplate as a prayer, praying it on their behalf and for their defence. It then becomes an all-embracing prayer of intercession.

The
Strong
Name
of the
Trinity

I bind unto myself today
The strong name of the Trinity,
By invocation of the same,
The Three in One and One in Three.

'I claim the truth of God as Trinity.' In the usual patterns of Christian teaching, this would be a strange starting-point. Most Christians who try to teach about the nature of God start with God as Creator, then go on to the doctrines concerning God the Son and God the Holy Spirit, then tie it all together in the doctrine of the Trinity. The Trinity appears as the conclusion of the whole story, and it can come across as the most puzzling part. The message that God is Three-in-One can appear to be mysterious obscurity, or mathematical nonsense.

But the Breastplate takes the Trinity as its starting-point. As in most Celtic songs and prayers, the Trinity is not a problem, but a blessing. Traditional Irish and Welsh symbolism delights in triads. Iolo Morgannwg's *The Triads of Britain* was published in Welsh in 1801. This book lists 126 instances of matters that occur in threes in British early history and legend – the three names given to the Isles of Britain being just one example. Many other things in human experience come in some sort of triple form, so why should God be different?

There is a blessing in this, at the start. According to much conventional thinking, things normally come in twos, in opposing pairs. The most universal opposition is that between the genders. To be 'normal', you have to be 100 per cent male or 100 per cent female. Male or female, young or old, rich or poor, straight or gay, classic or romantic, radical or conservative, extravert or introvert – everything gets polarized. We have to be in one position or the other – or, at least, we have to locate ourselves somewhere on a line between two extremes.

A  B

So we learn to be in opposition to one another, to exaggerate our standpoints and traditions, to identify ourselves in terms of our differences.

But if we start from the assumption that things come in threes, immediately we are in a much more interesting world. In a word, we have space.

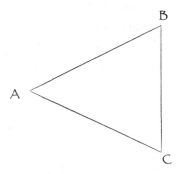

We no longer have to be located somewhere along one line; we can move around, we do not feel obliged to fit into an either/or choice, we are free. We do not have to identify ourselves in terms of our opposite. There is room for variety and difference. We can discover a secret of ecumenism, that Christians are generally right in what they affirm and wrong in what they deny. Christ is the 'Yes' to the many ways of responding to God's creative initiatives:

> . . . but in [Jesus Christ] it is always 'Yes.' For in him every one of God's promises is a 'Yes' (2 Corinthians 1.19–20).

In the Bible, the meaning of the names 'Joshua' and 'Jesus' is 'Saviour', and the underlying idea of 'Saviour' is the one who gives space. The God who saves is the God who is the spacious one, the space-maker. I bind myself to this God, who is the source of my freedom, who enables me to defy the pressures that would confine me into definitions

 and roles and rigid identities. Certainly, the Church always needs to be alert to what is wrong; it must always be an opposition party to the conformities of the world. But a spirituality that depends essentially on being in opposition will never satisfy, for churches that define themselves in terms of their difference to other groups will not nourish the human spirit, or hold our enthusiasm for long.

We believe that God is Three-in-One. How can we know? How can we know anything at all about the Creator of the universe? There may be ants crawling around under the doorstep of 10 Downing Street, but how can they get any idea of either the personal character or the professional policies of the Prime Minister? Can the Prime Minister become an ant? Can he share their life? Can he overcome the limitations of their information systems and language? If he could, perhaps the other ants wouldn't be able to stand him, and would destroy him. Then, even if he regained life, could he remain both ant and Prime Minister?

The difference between the Prime Minister and an ant is tiny compared to the difference between me (or even the Prime Minister) and our Creator. For one thing, the Prime Minister has not himself created either the ants or the doorstep. So, we are warned; any attempt to describe God is going to be very incomplete. But our symbol of the Trinity is one attempt, and it can build on the Celtic love of triads.

The Celtic image is typified in the design of three figures intertwined to make one. The male figure is for the Creator, the female figure is for the Spirit (a female noun in Hebrew), and the child figure is for the Son. In the Trinity, there is eternally the child. Of course, this does not pretend to be anything like a perfect likeness of God – just one tiny attempt at recognition.

God, Three-in-One, is diversity in unity. Father and Son and Spirit are eternally different, and eternally united. In our conventional understanding, power structures are like a pyramid; they work from above downwards, with a few in control at the top and many who are powerless at the bottom. To fit into this pattern, God would have to be a solo point of intense power, way up above the apex of the pyramid; the people who are at the top will be closest to God. This 'monarchic' image of God has been taken for granted among the powerful groups of people on earth to whom it is attractive and convenient. God and his (definitely **his!**) religious hierarchy, such groups assume, are in business to congratulate the powerful on being powerful.

But God as Trinity is not the lonely isolated one. God is community. At the heart of all things, the motive of power is subservient to the motive of love, the motive of competition is less real than the motive of co-operation, the motive of purity-by-exclusion is secondary to the motive of holiness-by-inclusion.

At the beginning of the day, I commit myself to this God.

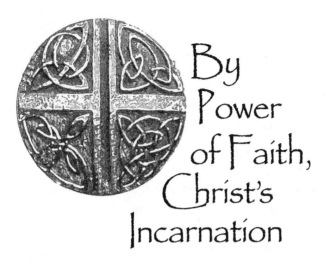

By Power of Faith, Christ's Incarnation

I bind this day to me for ever,
By power of faith, Christ's Incarnation;
His baptism in Jordan river;
His death on Cross for my salvation;
His bursting from the spiced tomb;
His riding up the heavenly way;
His coming at the day of doom;
I bind unto myself today.

'I bind to myself today Christ's incarnation.' Against much of the immediate evidence, I recognize that God has claimed this world as a fitting place for God to be in. God is no longer the remote one.

God is with us, among the many at the bottom of the power pyramid. On a day when I bind to myself the Incarnation of Christ, this is the God I will expect to find. I will watch for the Christ who was born into a family and community that had no voice and no vote, where the fruits of people's labour were being clawed back in tax and rent, to impoverish the poor and to enrich the privileged. I will seek to recognize a Christ who was very nearly born as child of a one-parent family, and who had to seek asylum in an unfriendly land. I will remember that all this story is told not in complaint or protest, but in praise of God's mercy in meeting us where we are.

I will celebrate the incarnation, God taking flesh, claiming the material and fleshly world as a fit dwelling-place, destroying the boundary between the holy and the earthly. In Jesus' time, meticulous religious people depended on this boundary for their identity. They needed to know who was **out** so that they could feel that they were **in**. Jesus defied this motive and subverted the religious boundaries, paying for this with his life. 'What was Jesus' greatest contribution to religion?' asked George MacLeod, Founder of the Iona Community. His answer: 'He abolished it.'

Later in the Breastplate, we pray for protection 'against false words of heresy'. This may sound like a matter of academic theology. 'Heresy', we assume, is a matter of a few bold people like Galileo, standing out against the static mind of the

Establishment. But in the earlier years of the Church, when the difference between truth and heresy was being worked out, the fundamental heresy was the refusal to accept that Jesus Christ had come **in the flesh**:

> . . . every spirit that confesses that Jesus Christ has come in the flesh is from God, and every spirit that does not confess Jesus is not from God (1 John 4.2–3).

All sorts of heresies were claiming, in one way or another, that the Son of God did not become a genuine human being, and that the gulf between God and humanity was too big for Christ to have crossed. And, as the First Letter of John makes clear, this is directly tied to the issue of whether we can truly love one another. If God has not really taken flesh in our real world, God remains simply the remote point of power, blessing and not challenging our conventional power systems. If Christ has not hallowed our human nature on earth, we can be content with a fellowship in heaven that makes no claim on our relationships on earth. This sort of heresy was a theological inspiration behind the policy of apartheid, and we need to pray to be defended against it wherever we are.

I bind to myself Christ's baptism. Jesus did not

set out from the start to be a radical revolutionary, disrupting all convention, scorning all tradition. He belonged; he took his place within a specific community, immersing himself in its culture and its attitudes. When he did make a move, he did not join any of the various pressure groups that were seeking to change things by attacking someone else, by blaming the Romans or the sinners or the political establishment or the modern urban culture. He associated himself with an old-fashioned prophet, who was giving the ordinary people of the land a chance to change things themselves. He joined John the Baptist, who preached a message of equality for the poor that could make sense even to a person who had only two coats:

> In reply he said to them, 'Whoever has two coats must share with anyone who has none; and whoever has food must do likewise' (Luke 3.11).

Jesus followed John down into the muddy and unprepossessing waters of the lower Jordan valley, for an even deeper immersion. He started where people were.

I bind myself to the crucified Christ. Christ was condemned by the best religion in the world and by the best law in the world. This was nothing out of the ordinary; Jesus died like all the others who challenged the ruling systems of the world. There was a vote. The general public was given the opportunity to choose between him and a bandit; it voted for Barabbas, unanimously. Jesus was executed by a method reserved for convicted terrorists and runaway slaves, and such executions were common enough for them to happen three at a time. The other two who were executed with him were convicted terrorists. All three were treated as human rubbish, superfluous, not required on this earth, ultimately and absolutely redundant. If I am redundant, I am in good company. If not, when I see people who are counted as expendable I will see them as people to whom Christ may be saying, 'Today you will be with me in Paradise'.

'God has made him both Lord and Messiah, this Jesus whom you crucified', so Peter preached on the Day of Pentecost (Acts 2.36 – for the whole sermon, read verses 22–38). This Jesus is the one who was carefully condemned by the responsible authorities and by the general public, but he was the one person on the scene for whom personal survival was less important than his commitment to the purposes of God. And so God has given him new life, raising him from the dead. If you can take this on board, if you can recognize that your whole way of making moral judgements is a mess, repent. But repentance doesn't mean feeling desperately guilty. As in the preaching of Jesus himself, repentance means there is a new opportunity; get up and take it. Don't just put up with the sad way that things are. Join our movement. Be baptized and together we will turn the world around.

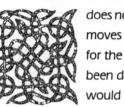

Jesus remains the crucified one. Resurrection does not merely turn the clock back. Jesus moves on, visibly damaged. I will watch for the signs of a God whose hands have been damaged by nails, as my own hand would be damaged if someone drove a nail through it. Thus disabled, he remains one of us. He takes our human nature into the community of eternity, into the nature of God's self. Anything that now devalues our humanity, any treating of persons as expendable, or as rubbish, or as a joke, is not just bad manners; it is not even merely criminal. It is blasphemy.

We will not escape judgement, but the one who is to judge us has a qualification that most human judges have not acquired. He has himself been on the receiving end of the most fundamental human judgement. He has been condemned to death; he knows, from inside, the processes of law, of custom, of definition, that lead to people being condemned. He will not easily fit into our preconceptions. He will not condemn what we would like to see condemned or condone what we would like to see condoned. Jesus has shown already how he behaves as judge. In his judgement, he counted as fit to join him at table all sorts of people who were classed as unacceptable by the representatives of religion. He did not wait for them to become respectable; he treated them as friends. His judgement does not grind failures deeper into failure; it is new creation. The systems of the world would classify people according to their quality, but Jesus' judgement exposes the systems of the world as forms of enmity towards God's own nature. I bind myself today to seeing our world and its people in the light of all that Jesus is and all that Jesus means. He does not give definitions or rules, but we may be able sometimes to see how his vision of the world can steer our own small vision.

Jesus is coming, among us. If he were only justice, or truth, or beauty, or morality, it might be possible to say that the revelation is complete, that there is nothing more to add. But, beyond all else, and however incomplete our understanding of it, Jesus, Son of God and Son of Mary, is ultimately summed up in one word: love. And love is never complete and finished. If there is love, there must be more to come.

Our
Community
Beyond
this World

I bind unto myself the power
Of the great love of Cherubim;
The sweet 'Well done' in judgement hour;
The service of the Seraphim,
Confessors' faith, Apostles' word,
The Patriarchs' prayers, the Prophets'
scrolls,
All good deeds done unto the Lord,
And purity of virgin souls.

I bind to myself. I take responsibility for myself, first person singular, but I do so in solidarity with a vast community of obedience and commitment. The Breastplate is all about companionship.

When I was in charge of a missionary training college in Birmingham, one of our students from

Latin America told us that he was very impressed by the Church of England, because 'the services always start on time, irrespective of whether the Holy Spirit has arrived or not'. Yes, we may be regulated by the clock, but in truth when we commence an act of worship we are not starting anything, any more than we are starting anything when we switch on a programme on the radio or pick up our e-mails. Something is already going on, and we merely connect into it.

The worship of the angels is going on all the time, and at the Eucharist we join with the angels and archangels and all the company of heaven. And, at a literally more mundane level, the same is true of our more domestic community on earth.

As o'er each continent and island
The dawn leads on another day,
The voice of prayer is never silent
Nor dies the strain of praise away.[1]

Our awareness of geography puts us into solidarity with colleagues in other parts of the world across time. The worship of the Jewish temple provided for a 24-hour programme of praise – 'You that by night stand in the house of the Lord, lift up your hands in the sanctuary and bless the Lord.' And the response comes from the sacred night-shift: 'May the Lord . . . bless you from Zion' (Psalm 134.3). I remember this every night, in community with our colleagues in the suffering and witnessing Church of the modern Jerusalem, along with so many others, of different traditions, who are yearning for peace in the Holy City. The worldwide Church offers a 24-hour programme of devotion. Wherever you are and whatever you are doing, there will be some community somewhere where people are breaking the bread and lifting up their hearts in praise, praying for the whole community of God's people – and that includes you.

If this is true of the little fragment we call the Church on earth, it is even more true of the wider community of God's servants. In South Africa, when I was newly appointed to a group of churches in an African community, I went to make a first visit to one of the local catechists. He showed me the little church building where he regularly led worship, then he said, 'Would you like to see our other church?' 'Yes, of course', I said, expecting to be taken to another church building. He led me to the graveyard. For him, this was a place of real people, a place where something was going on, a place of obedience and discovery.

So at the beginning of a new day I bind myself to

the community of worship and obedience that has been going on all the time. That wider community of God's servants sustains those who have died, those of us who are alive in this life, and – a matter of value to us as we worry about the kind of world that we are handing on to our grandchildren – those who are still unborn. I join in the flow; I switch myself into the on-going programme; I shift a gear and drive into a movement that is eternal.

The saints are with us. These are not only the ones who name the name of Christ; their list includes the patriarchs and prophets of the Hebrew Scriptures, people like Abraham, Jacob, Ruth, Isaiah and Jeremiah; they were obedient to God's will before the coming of Christ. Amid a swirl of false prophets, for whom 'God' was just a national idol, these prophets realized that God must also be the God of the enemy. We honour them in company with our old cousins the Jews, and with those other children of Abraham, the Muslims. And there are good deeds done, in honesty and purity, in even wider circles. There are people who will be surprised to be told that, in caring for their fellow human beings, they have been caring for the Son of God (Matthew 25.31–46). They will have been on the side of the deepest truth about the creation. They are all part of the flow of obedience, of searching, of communion.

A few years ago, my wife and I were invited to the consecration of a bishop in the Roman Catholic Communion. In many ways the service was very similar to that of my own consecration, but in the middle there was a long litany of the saints, inviting the prayers of scores of holy persons whose heroic sanctity had been publicly acknowledged by the Church. At the end, we looked at each other and agreed: 'If he's got all those on his side, he can't go wrong!'

One of the most memorable people I have known was a woman of about my own age called Eva. Coming as a Jew from Central Europe, she had known the horrors of her people's experience under Nazism. She had nursed in India, survived the Mau Mau terrors of East Africa, and had pioneered a new form of pastoral ministry in an English university. With this wide experience, she came to us in South Africa to dedicate herself to the struggle against racism, injustice and poverty. With great vitality and generous humour, she gained the trust and respect of all kinds of people. She was a breath of fresh air in a very discouraging scene. She lived next door to us in Johannesburg. But after only a few months, and while still in her forties, she was diagnosed as suffering from incurable cancer. She had to leave South Africa and go to London. Soon after, but for quite different reasons, my family and I also found ourselves as exiles in London. For Eva and ourselves, there was a painful question, 'Had we got it all wrong?' What was the purpose? As death approached, Eva felt and looked very depressed. Then she was given a vision. Thousands of people who had suffered through the persecution of Jews, through Mau Mau, through racial oppression, were beckoning to her from 'the other side'; they were putting their reserves of courage, their accumulated credit of faith, at her disposal. With all this on her side, she won. As she described the vision, she started to breathe freely again, to speak with her old vitality. The wretched dead colour left her; she looked and sounded vigorous and young and ready for anything. A few hours later she died – or departed, or arrived, or however you like to express it. And now she is one of the millions of God's servants who can offer the same sort of resource for us, as we bind ourselves into solidarity with them – now, and at the hour of our death. Amen.

In the Middle Ages, they called this idea the Treasury of Merit. It then became commercialized and discredited, and was dropped from our standard kitbag of symbols. But Eva found it for real, and it is what we celebrate at every Eucharist. George MacLeod used to say that the island of Iona is 'a thin place', a place where the boundary between earth and heaven is transparent. It certainly does feel to be true of Iona. But every Christian altar is really a thin place, where we meet with the angels and archangels and all the company of heaven.

Blessed Patrick, and all our companions, pray for us.

Note

1 Verse 3 of hymn 252 in *The New English Hymnal* (Norwich, Canterbury Press, 1986).

I Belong in God's Creation

I bind unto myself today
The virtues of the starlit heaven,
The glorious sun's life-giving ray,
The whiteness of the moon at even,
The flashing of the lightning free,
The whirling wind's tempestuous shocks,
The stable earth, the deep salt sea,
Around the old eternal rocks.

St Patrick, and Mrs Alexander, had one advantage over modern urban folk: they lived before our era of electric light. For them, 'the virtues of the starlit heaven' would be much more accessible than for most of us today. We have to try to see the stars past a wasteful pollution of badly designed streetlamps and carelessly adjusted floodlights. But we still belong in this vast universe; we can bind it to ourselves, trusting in the innumerable coincidences and fine tunings, identified by physicists and chemists, that make our existence possible. I commit myself to the planet that mothers me. I affirm my responsibility for treasuring and respecting it in its variety and fragility.

The position of this verse in the Breastplate is exactly true to Christian belief about the world of nature. First, we celebrate God as Trinity, then we recognize God in the person and work of Jesus Christ, the Lord of all creation. And after this, with Christ, we celebrate our place within the creation. The Celtic tradition from which the Breastplate comes is enthusiastic in celebrating the natural world. This is profoundly different to that very common kind of spirituality that suggests that you can get closer to God by putting yourself at a distance from this physical and material world, the world of things, of finance, of sex. That kind of spirituality denies all that we mean by incarnation. It was within the natural world, the world of work and construction and bargaining, that the incarnate Son of God found his place. Without that world, he would have had nothing from which to construct his parables.

These powers of nature are my companions. I

bind myself to them, recognizing that they and I are of the same stuff. Because they are, I can be. But they cannot know me, so I do not worship them. The poorest child has infinitely more consciousness than the most sublime star. The child can know something of the star; the star can know nothing of the child. However marvellous may be the discoveries of modern physics, the most extraordinary thing in physics is still the physicist. But I acknowledge these material things as part of what I also am part of. They were around long before me and will be there long after me. I and my mammalian cousins are very recent arrivals. I recognize also that, at first sight, the environment is not entirely friendly. From my limited point of view, some of the natural processes may be terrifying and destructive. There's a wildness in God's mercy, like the wildness of the sea. The lightning flashes free without reference to my safety or convenience. The same is true of the whirling wind and the shifting of tectonic plates. The earth itself is indeed 'stable', in that most of the time we can rely on it staying put and enabling fruitfulness. But in fact it is always on the move; unless there were earthquakes – with the risk of tsunamis – the mountains would have eroded long ago; we should have a planet with a smooth crust, covered evenly by hundreds of fathoms of water; this might be fine for cod, but we would have to wait an eternity for chips.

The natural forces and I are part of the same creative process. My body, like yours, and like the body of Jesus, is made of the dust of dead stars. We are in one family together, so we can know the great things of nature, as St Francis did, as Brother Sun, Sister Moon, and even as Sister Death.

The things of nature are created as things that are good in themselves; they are not merely things for me to exploit or play with. Still less are they commodities for me to claim a stake in, to own, in competition with other people. When I start the day with this prayer, I am committing myself to the Creator. I will look around and sing:

> The earth is the Lord's and all that is in it,
> the world, and those who live in it (Psalm 24.1).

With eyes open to this commitment, I will look at my house, my street, my work, my wealth, the products that I use. Above all, I will look at the land, the 'stable earth'. This is one thing that humans did not make and cannot make. Yet we deal with it as if it were just another commodity, to be divided up and claimed in competition with one another. We lament that the price of 'property' has been anything but stable. It staggers out of control; sometimes it leaps up, so that young people cannot buy their own homes; sometimes it plummets down and traps owners in negative equity. But it is not the cost of building materials, or of labour, that has been so erratic. It is the value placed on land itself. The land is our common home, under the Creator; but it has become part of a financial game, played by those who have got wealth to spare. Most wars have been fought on the question of who shall have control of the land; and where this is the case, the 'peace' that follows turns out to be a device for continuing the war by other methods. So I will seek to recognize that the earth and the wealth that comes from it are all on loan to us, to the whole human race, and not merely to those who have managed to grasp the levers of control.

There is a touching comment, repeated several times, in the Book of Judges that, after a period of conflict and destruction, 'the land had rest for forty years'. In our culture, a skyscraper is demolished and replaced by a taller skyscraper; should not that bit of land have a rest from carrying the absurd loads that ambitious human beings place upon it? But that would not fit in with our understanding of land as 'property'. 'The stable earth', yes, but like the glorious sun and the bright moon, its blessing is for all equally. If we treat the earth as simply a source of plunder, where the privileged can grasp as much as they can, and our status is measured by the size of our carbon footprint, the earth's stability will be betrayed; the environment has its own way of affirming its rights. The whirling wind's tempestuous shocks will not be only the outworking of the checks and balances built into the natural order; they will be evidence of a disturbing of the equilibrium of nature; and human activity will bear some responsibility. Environmental changes tend to do most damage where many people are poor and are living on vulnerable coastlines. The way we treat the earth is a mirror of what we do to our fellow human beings, and it shows what we think of the rights of those who are yet to be born.

This is one of the verses of the Breastplate that are 'starred' in the older hymn books – that is, to be treated as optional – and that are totally omitted in newer ones. St Patrick and Mrs Alexander, as people of Celtic lands, would be dismayed. If we don't get our commitment to the Creator right, we shall have nothing for the sacraments of redemption to claim and work on. The things that we use in the sacraments are representative. They are the small things that stand for the whole. For instance, the Christian community builds a building that it calls

'God's house', a structure that is accessible for all, not limited just to those who 'own' it, or pay for it; not reserved only for a group of people who have devised convenient ways of excluding other people. 'God's house' is representative, declaring that all houses are God's. The water of baptism is blessed, to declare that all water is of God's creation. The bread of the Eucharist is the holy bread, to declare that all bread is holy. We take the bread and wine, 'which earth has given and human hands have made', to claim the holiness of all creation, both the natural and the industrial.

There are some who would say that this kind of vision is unrealistic, too romantic, too much like a New Age outlook that is fine for those who have the freedom to trust in nice smells and pretty flowers, but is useless for those who are ground down by the cruelties of this world. But it should work the other way round. The water of baptism is directly connected to the water that is scarce for so many in our world. The bread of Eucharist is connected to the bread for lack of which so many starve. The sacraments insist that 'the earth is the Lord's'; and where the things of the earth are not shared under the Lord's authority, the servants of God are to struggle to discover the signs of the kingdom. Jesus showed what it means for God to be incarnate: being incarnate means being vulnerable to the place where you find yourself. That discipline applies to us, as we try to be the Body of Christ, the incarnate God, in our day and place, at a time when the future existence of our planet is at last becoming a live political issue. When cholera was wreaking its deadly ruin on the lives of Londoners, Canon Henry Scott Holland of St Paul's summed up his faith: 'The more you believe in the Incarnation, the more you care about drains.' That's a fair summary of the meaning of Christmas. The more we really believe in it, the more we will seek to change the current way of the world, in which the rich are stealing the earth's wealth from the poor, the present generation from the yet to be born.

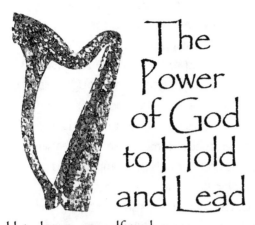

The Power of God to Hold and Lead

I bind unto myself today
The power of God to hold and lead,
God's eye to watch, God's might to stay,
God's ear to hearken to my need.
The wisdom of my God to teach,
God's hand to guide, God's shield to ward;
The word of God to give me speech,
God's heavenly host to be my guard.

The original text of the Breastplate refers to God as 'pilot'. Who, for us, are 'pilots'? In these days, for most people in the UK, they are people in neat uniforms, carrying briefcases along airport corridors and through the departure lounges. We won't see them again; we will just hear a reassuring voice describing the weather at 35,000 feet. We will trust the pilot to steer us clear of storms and cumulonimbus, and to cope with disorderly passengers and the threat of hijackers. But my own first picture of a 'pilot' is of a man in oilskins, stepping from a tiny boat in a choppy sea off Point Lynas in Anglesey, or at the Bar Lightship on the Mersey, climbing up a rope ladder on to the deck of a huge ship. His task will be to navigate the ship with his own special competence, to steer her past the hazards and through the complications of the port's shipping lane, and to bring her to dock or landing-stage. The ship's officers stay on board, but they submit themselves to the pilot's authority and hand over the use of the navigational equipment and controls.

The people of God who first prayed the Breastplate did not know of pilots in either of these two senses, but they knew plenty about the hazards of navigation. Their communication with other places was more by sea than by land in those days, so I reckon that they would identify with the seafarers' idea of 'pilot'. At the beginning of the day, we pause deliberately to allow God's authority to come on board. God is with us. God in Christ knows what this world is like, with its hazards and its landmarks. We commit ourselves to God as navigator for the day.

The pilot is our guide for a journey; each new day involves crossing a boundary, a frontier into new and unexplored territory. I live near Offa's Dyke; in the Middle Ages, this was the longest man-made border in Europe. Nearby is Llangollen, the venue for an annual international music festival, which is one of the most remarkable boundary-crossing enterprises in Britain. In 1946, people in Llangollen were asking, 'What can we Welsh people do to help to heal the terrible wounds that the world has been inflicting on itself during this century?' Their answer was the founding of the Llangollen International Musical Eisteddfod. For over 60 years, groups of singers and dancers from all over the world have been meeting in friendly competition, crossing every kind of barrier of language, political identity and religious commitment. In 2004, the Eisteddfod was on the shortlist for the Nobel Prize for Peace. In 2003, a poet, Grahame Davies, was commissioned to write a set of poems in Welsh and English to celebrate the Eisteddfod. The first verse of the first poem reads:

Man cwrdd, neu fan cau allan ydyw'r ffin;
Â chraith Clawdd Offa'n hollti'r fro yn ddwy
Eiddo pob enaid byw yn dewis p'un.[1]

(The border can release you or confine.

With Offa's Dyke dividing the land in two,
Every soul must choose that walks the line.)

The border, says the poet, can be a place of
meeting or a barrier. Where a border like Offa's
Dyke divides the land in two, everyone can make
the choice. The boundary into a new day can be a
meeting-place, with God and with other people,
with our environment and with ourselves; or it can
be a dead-end. The servant of God is a natural
frontier-person, a professional wall-puncturer. Our
business is to recognize and confront all the
unwarranted forms of exclusion and exclusiveness
that human beings set up against one another.

The previous verse of the Breastplate celebrates
the creation; and from the creation my eye and my
commitment are led to the Creator. As Christians,
our understanding of creation will be informed by
the discoveries of science, but it will not be limited to
them. Our Creator is not only the one who creates
and maintains the natural order; he is known as
'Creator' because he creates a new nation out of
a collection of runaway slaves, and intervenes
to give responsibility and value to those who are
disregarded and disinherited. At the heart of the
universe there is not just an impersonal force or
even a designing mind. There is One who knows

the road, who is a reliable source of protection and wisdom. God is eye and ear and hand and speech. Comparatively speaking, I am blind, deaf, crippled, dumb – and have great learning difficulties. The differences between me and those who carry the official label 'disabled' are insignificant. In belonging to society and the Church, I am just a member of a patients' co-operative. If any person is excluded, I am excluded too. But God is on our side; God enables us in our 'dis-ability'. God claims us with such abilities as we have, to use in co-operation with the abilities of our fellow pilgrims. There are other companions, whose physical speech and vision and hearing may be 'normal', but whose voices are not heard, who are kept out of the official communication systems, who get little opportunity to move around or to take responsibility for the world where they are placed, who are labelled as 'problems'. God in Christ is with these people in their dis-ability also.

As I move into the day, I do so in company with Christ. Christ, the representative of God, might appear to be the one whose speech, vision and hearing are perfect. From his example, we might think that God's perfection merely emphasizes the second-class character of people with dis-abilities. But Christ was blindfolded, was not listened to, was pinned down immobile, was reckoned to be stupid or crazy; he now carries the scars caused by those who treated him as expendable. God knows disability from the inside. To quote Bonhoeffer, 'Christ has come as our Brother, and wants no honour for himself as long as his sisters or brothers are dishonoured.'[2]

Science can seem to be a device for congratulating clever people on being clever, and religion may seem to be a device for congratulating good people on being good. An authoritarian Church may seem to be a device for congratulating powerful people on being powerful. To the stupid, the dis-abled, the immoral, the slave, the word of the true God breaks through: 'Congratulations to you! You are made in the image of God. The Son of God is your brother.' So, whoever I am, I move into this day with this kind of status to empower me, this kind of vision to inspire me, this kind of awareness to hear me, this kind of companionship to support me, this kind of presence to protect me.

Notes

1 The complete sequence of poems by Grahame Davies is published in *A World in Harmony* (© Friends of Llangollen International Musical Eisteddford, Royal International Pavilion, Abbey Road, Llangollen LL20 8NG, 2005). Quoted by permission of the author.

2 Dietrich Bonhoeffer, *The Cost of Discipleship* (London, SCM Press, 1959), p.117.

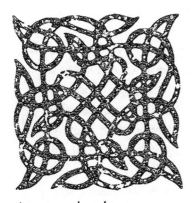

Holy Powers

Against the demon snares of sin,
The vice that gives temptation force,
The natural lusts that war within,
The hostile men that mar my course,
Or few or many, far or nigh,
In every place and in all hours,
Against their fierce hostility,
I bind to me these holy powers.

We have committed ourselves to God, to God as Trinity, to God in flesh in Christ, to the powers of God in the spirits of those who are bonded to God's realm, to the whole created order, and to God in relationship to ourselves. This is all a positive beginning to the day; we do not start with our sense of things being wrong, with original sin, with the claims of our guilt. But the Breastplate is not just for people who can sit easily in the world as it is. It does not ignore the darkness. In the faith that we have been celebrating thus far, we can reckon with the enemy. Two more verses of the Breastplate follow, which are optional in the older hymn books and omitted in the new. But without these verses, the Breastplate is like a kitchen without a sink – it may look more hygienic, but it won't have the equipment to deal with disorder and defilement. Just at a time when we are more than ever conscious of the terrors of the world, our prayer books and hymnbooks are chopping away the old prayers for deliverance that we could claim in the struggle.

Within the good creation, things go wrong in three ways. The third and most substantial way is dealt with in the verse that follows, which we turn to in the next chapter. In this verse, we recognize two sources. First, there are the conflicts and contradictions within myself, the motives that St Paul describes so graphically in Romans 7 as the evil that I do that I do not want to do:

So I find it to be a law that when I want to do what is good, evil lies close at hand . . . Wretched man that I am! (Romans 7.21–24).

We can find a comparison from the hydraulic system of any modern vehicle. The driver puts a slight pressure on the brake pedal; this is boosted by energy from the servo mechanism, and the result is a force that can cause a heavy vehicle to stop. 'The vice which gives temptation force' in the prayer works in the same sort of way. A little pressure, a little suggestion from my own heart, triggers a whole lot of active energy from other sources and I find myself involved in the committing of some kind of sin. I cannot always predict this sort of thing, so at the beginning of the day I claim the powers of the Creator's success to obstruct this process.

Second, there are the forces of evil that come at me through people, and I need to be realistic about them. If I am to love my enemies, I first need to acknowledge that this is what they are. Faced, for instance, with Major S and Captain B of the South African Security Police during my time as a priest in Johannesburg, it would be foolish to pretend that they were anything other than 'hostile men'. They certainly marred my course. Captain B gave me a wretched time in repeated interrogations, and gave far worse to many others, especially black Africans. I believe that these two men, more than anyone else, were responsible for me being unable to continue working in South Africa. I claim the protection of divine power against the likes of them, on my own behalf and representing the other victims. Once during a particularly nasty confrontation, my wife noticed that Captain B wore a wedding ring. Somewhere out there, there was a woman who loved him. And of course he was also a victim of a system that he could neither create nor destroy. Paul says in his Letter to the Ephesians:

> For our struggle is not against enemies of blood and flesh, but against the rulers, against the authorities, against the cosmic powers of this present darkness (Ephesians 6.12).

Our battle is against the superhuman forces of evil that trap and corrupt the human spirit and frustrate the blessings of the Creator. One of the most urgent spiritual disciplines is to learn how to oppose evil without becoming an instrument of evil oneself. If we hope to succeed, it must be on the understanding that our enemy will have as secure a place as we ourselves, in the future order of things. So, I must claim the powers of truth and justice on behalf of the likes of Captain B as well as my own.

It is, perhaps, too easy for me to quote grotesque examples of evil, such as Major S and Captain B, who were well known for their brutality. For most of the time and in most places, the forces of evil will be more devious and concealed, more crafted to catch the unwary. It was while I was in Britain, in an autumnal October, that I had to accept that I was not going to be able to continue with any ministry in South Africa. But I have never thought that Britain was an easier option. I wrote to friends to say that in both countries there were difficulties. South Africa was a country in which it was difficult to see one's way forward, because it was a land of darkness. Britain also was a country in which it was difficult to see one's way forward, because it was a land of fog. But in the darkness one can see stars, which is more than can be said for the fog. There certainly were stars amid the violence that was the darkness of South Africa; the light of some of them has since shone across the world. In the fog of acquisitiveness, of exclusiveness, of complacency, it is easier to be caught unawares, to be co-opted into a culture that assumes, for instance, that the violence of the world can be cured by killing people, or that the natural environment can look after itself and we can just go on exploiting it.

So, Mrs Alexander's version of the Breastplate bids us claim the protection of God's powers 'at every place and in all hours'. This echoes a central phrase of the eucharistic prayer; 'at all times and in all places' we will recognize the presence and the claim of God, we will make thanksgiving, we will celebrate our identity in community; and this will not be limited to times and places organized by formal church councils. Every table will be a meeting-place with God; every piece of bread will speak to us of the One Body.

Note

In all of Mrs Alexander's version of the Breastplate, there is just one place where I would question her interpretation, namely at the word 'natural' in line 3 of this verse – 'the natural lusts that war within'. (This is Mrs Alexander's emphasis; it is not required by the Celtic original.) Certainly, I need to claim the powers of holiness to confront in me the egocentric lusts and fantasies of greed, of censoriousness, of sloth, of defensiveness, of sullen pride. But are these motives **natural** lusts? Are they not, rather, diseases and deformities? Are they 'natural' to the humanity that is being created by God, that was claimed by Christ in his incarnation, and has been eternally reclaimed in his resurrection? I have tried over 60 alternative words that might fit both the meaning and the metre; of these, 'devious' is the closest to what I feel to be true about myself. I had thought about simply sliding in this word to replace 'natural', without comment. But this did not seem quite honest, and then I thought of what might be called the 'Huxley' options. With early twentieth-century scientific optimism, the eminent biologist Sir Julian Huxley reckoned that natural evolution could provide a proper basis for human behaviour. His grandfather, Thomas, colleague of Darwin, was more gloomy, more realistic, and therefore more hopeful. He claimed that the ethical progress of society would depend not on imitating the natural drives of evolution, but on combating them. What price the 'natural', in that case? See again how Paul struggles with this dilemma in Romans 7. For me, as a child of Adam and a child of God, the question remains open. Reluctantly, I'm sticking with Mrs Alexander's version, and I hope that creation-affirming Celts will understand.

Protect Me, Christ

Against all Satan's spells and wiles,
Against false words of heresy,
Against the knowledge that defiles,
Against the heart's idolatry,
Against the wizard's evil craft,
Against the death-wound and the burning,
The choking wave, the poisoned shaft,
Protect me, Christ, till thy returning.

Anyone who has been caught up in the struggle against cruel and heretical ideologies, such as racism, will know that evil works at a level much wider than that of individual choice. The power of evil conceals and corrupts what is good. It depends on what is good, just as forged currency depends on good currency. The good comes first; that is why all the positive and affirming verses come first in the Breastplate. Evil is everywhere; it is powerful and terrifying. But it is not simply the eternal equal and opposite of good. 'Satan' is as good a label as any for this power of evil, even if today our experience of evil is on such a massive scale that the traditional

figure of 'Satan' looks absurdly trivial. In the Book of Job, Satan prowls around the world, spying on people's misbehaviours. (Some scholars think that the figure of Satan was inspired by the activities of the Persian empire's secret intelligence agency.) Satan's influence distorts the motives of those who seek to oppose evil, so that we start to want our opponents to be worse than they actually are. If we are in business to oppose the government, anything good that government does will be bad news. We set ourselves up as prosecutors; and we thus become agents of Satan ourselves. So Satan is not just a free-moving spirit, catching vulnerable individuals. Satan is the spiritual bundle of motives that steer human structures when they become enslaved to delusions and idolatry. In the Gospel story of the temptations, Satan quotes the truth to manipulate Christ away from the truth. Satan makes truth untrue, trying to claim material power, political power and religious power to subvert Christ's obedience. In this one series of conversations, we are shown the kind of fantasies that can lead us into untruth, as citizens and people of religion (Luke 4.1–13). We call on Christ to defend us, because Christ has shown that Satan has power only when untruth is allowed to take control.

Large-scale evil seems to encourage witchcraft in the narrower sense to flourish. Out of malice, or in a perverse delight in experimentation, people try to manipulate spiritual powers to dominate or control other people. Against all this, we claim the protection of Christ the exorcist. This was close to us in ministry in South Africa. But in the Welsh/English borderlands where I have lived for the last 20 years there are areas that have been fought over for centuries. When I was a bishop in Shropshire I was more directly involved in exorcism than at any time since leaving Africa. I have no special expertise; I was doing an ordinary priest's job. My equipment has been simply the sign of the cross, holy water, and St Patrick's Breastplate – not just these combative verses, but the whole song that celebrates God's success as well as confronting the powers that we have to defy.

Christ's ministry as exorcist was not confined to those occasions when he was specifically casting out demons. The evangelists do not classify the acts of Jesus into exorcisms, healings, confrontations, and so on. The whole ministry of Jesus was a continuous succession of attacks on the powers that reduced people's confidence in God and in their own humanity. The healing of a paralytic was as much an occasion of salvation as the restoration of Zacchaeus, the affirmation of the acceptability of the haemorrhaging woman was as much an attack on the powers of darkness as the healing of a leper.

The teaching ministry of Jesus was itself a kind of exorcism, an attack on the mind-set that enslaved people to untruths concerning holiness, the character of God, and their own unacceptability. He attacked a spirituality that gave preference to the fittest, and declared a realm of God in which the weak, the outcast, and the excluded would have priority. This too is exorcism: a casting out of the heart's idolatry.

If ever I get connected to the internet, I will pin to my computer this verse, claiming protection 'against the knowledge that defiles' – one of Mrs Alexander's most cunning phrases. Certainly, modern information technology has brought great benefits, but it also deals in the knowledge that defiles, including corruptions such as child pornography; it encourages the insatiable demands of consumerism, the grabbing of more and more resources, the stimulation of dissatisfaction. It stirs the heart to idolatry. Where knowledge is valued as a means of restricting resources to those who are in on the secret, where knowledge is not openly shared, it itself becomes defiled. The knowledge industry today depends on huge financial investment; this is its essential resource, and perhaps its greatest danger. Technology itself will not save us. You have to have adequate technology to be a competent criminal. Indeed, modern technology can, by its very nature, reinforce the delusion that if you can get the numbers right you can put everything right. One of Satan's little tricks was to get government to trust in statistics:

> Satan stood up against Israel, and incited David to count the people of Israel (1 Chronicles 21.1).

Evil enterprises rely on good communication.

Today's culture emphasizes the value of choice; it invites us all the time to choose things that will suit us, whether we think of food or schools or vehicles or political programmes or sexual partners. Poor people are made to feel even poorer by being confronted by 'choice' between shelves stacked full of items that they cannot afford, which are distinguished from each other only by the label. It is like the old proposal, 'Would you prefer to be

eaten by a lion called Leo or by a lion called Cleo?'
In religion, especially in urban areas, we can look
around and select a church that suits us. This may
be a church that makes least demand on us to think
or change – one that will protect us against any
danger of conversion. In finding a church that suits
us, we are in danger of finding a god who suits us, a
god who will allow us to press on with our schemes
of self-interest and of control. The technical term
for a god who suits us is 'idol'. This idol will stand
up for our interests in opposition to the interests
of others. So each nation and interest group will
have its idol; in the Bible, idolatry is a much greater
danger than atheism. But Christ refuses to be an
idol; we can be sure that Christ will not suit us. We
pray that Christ will, on this day and through us,
continue his disruption of the order and the peace
that we find convenient.

Evil is all around us, not just in the obviously
evil actions of conspicuous individuals, but in the
organizations in which we live and work. If we
have the time, the language and the inclination,
we may perhaps ponder this and argue about it.
The first Christian communities did not have the
time; they did not seek an interpretation of evil.
They did not pray, 'Help us to understand evil', but
'Deliver us from evil'; they knew that persecution

was just around the corner. But this prayer was not a magical incantation, nor is the Breastplate. God is not necessarily a solution in a crisis; the prayers of the terrorists on 9/11 were answered, the prayers of those about to die on the aircraft were not. The old servants of God before Jesus's time knew of these things:

> If our God whom we serve is able to deliver us from the furnace of blazing fire and out of your hand, O king, let him deliver us. But if not, be it known to you, O king, that we will not serve your gods and we will not worship the golden statue that you have set up (Daniel 3.17–18).

We will maintain our commitment to the truth, even if fantasy, idolatry or delusion are enthroned. Real choice is possible.

The traditional wizard is a paid servant of the powers that dominate the world. This is true of the magus of the New Testament and of the modern African sorcerer. His evil craft is a reality for millions of people; it involves the conscious manipulation of people's credulity. It means claiming secret skills and arcane information, to be used for the advantage of those who can control the systems and for the disadvantage of those who can't. It means deriving exploitable information from good material things, from physical symptoms and measurable data, and using them to steer people's feelings and choices. Anyone who has lived close to traditional 'witchcraft' will recognize these features. The Christian gospel has been welcomed by people who have been burdened under this sort of witchcraft; the mysteries of the Christian altar are open and equal for all, and are received as a profound blessing. The Breastplate does not encourage a romantic cosiness about religious witchcraft.

But witchcraft is not confined to 'primitive' communities. Its basic features of manipulation and victimization are all around us: in science, journalism, economics, international relations, education, law and government – and religious organizations are certainly not exempt. These are all good things, but they can be co-opted into the service of the lie. We need to ask: Who is getting the benefit, and in what direction are resources being moved? Towards sharing and compassion? Or towards the maintenance of delusions, of structures that exclude and deny our common humanity? You can test election manifestos by these criteria, but don't assume that you can change things by staying outside the systems and firing off trenchant criticisms. Jesus was no escapee from the structures of his day. The real servants of the truth include those who get critically involved with such enterprises as local government and financial management, and who work with the world's powers from within. If this is your particular calling today, claim the defence of Christ as you enter territory that is in danger of being claimed by the enemy. And remember there must be a place even for the wizard in God's final reconciliation.

The wizard deals in knowledge that is defiled. Robert Oppenheimer was the leader of the team of nuclear physicists who developed the atomic bomb in the USA, and after the first testing in 1945 in the desert of New Mexico, he confessed: 'Physicists have now known sin.' And this was **before** the bomb was actually used against human populations. What happened next is only too familiar – the poisoned missile, the choking wave, the burning, the death-wound. The Breastplate sums up Hiroshima and Nagasaki in three lines. The wizard's evil craft is our global threat. Protect us, Christ, and use us to protect one another. Call us to resistance to such wizardry, that it may be driven from the earth. Confound the plans of those who seek to acquire such power for themselves, and redirect the energies of those who seek to update or 'improve' the systems that they already possess.

Protect us, Christ; return to us, to your stupid and destructive people.

Christ Within Me

Christ be with me, Christ within me,
Christ behind me, Christ before me,
Christ beside me, Christ to win me,
Christ to comfort and restore me,
Christ beneath me, Christ above me,
Christ in quiet, Christ in danger,
Christ in hearts of all that love me,
Christ in mouth of friend and stranger.

Mrs Alexander's version moves into a new metre for this verse, and it becomes a prayer on its own. When the Breastplate is sung as a hymn, this verse has its own melody, a melody that, like the melody of the other verses, is marvellously appropriate.

But this verse should not be isolated from the rest of the Breastplate. We have had two verses that realistically face the threats and dreads that confront us, and this present verse provides necessary resources to enable us to face the reality of what has gone before. It flows on directly from the prayers for protection, and enables our defiance.

 We are all familiar with a world of three dimensions, of up and down, side to side, in front and behind. It makes sense to think also of time as a fourth dimension. But modern physics is suggesting that there may be 11 or more dimensions. I cannot envisage them, and I do not claim to understand what they are about. But dimensions are ways in which things are in relationship to one another, and this verse of the Breastplate suggests about 15 ways of Christ's relatedness to us, 15 dimensions. Some of them are dimensions of space – before, behind, beneath, above. Others are dimensions of function – to win, to comfort. And others are dimensions of my own position and my relationships – in quiet and danger, in the hearts and on the lips of other people. They are all bundled together, in typical Celtic creative confusion.

This is a prayer for pilgrims, people on the move. One translation of the original of the Breastplate sees the pilgrim as on a journey by sea – 'Christ in my headway, Christ in my wake'. Christ is alongside us, with us as our companion. But first of all, Christ is **in** us; he moves into the immeasurable space that is me. I do not know it fully. What I, or anyone else, can say about me is less than what cannot be said. The inside is larger than the outside. This is true of any person; even more it is true of Christ, of God. Part of our honouring of one another is this humble willingness not to know. When the powerful feel that they **know** people, then they start to claim the right to control them; and that is the beginning of tyranny. This is not only a matter of large-scale politics; it is true between spouses, between parents and children. When people thought that they **knew** Jesus, that was the place where no change or mercy was possible:

> He left that place and came to his home town, and his disciples followed him. On the sabbath he began to teach in the synagogue, and many who heard him were astounded. They said, 'Where did this man get all this? What is this wisdom that has been given to him? What deeds of power are being done by his hands! Is not this the carpenter, the son of Mary and brother of James and Joses and Judas and Simon, and are not his sisters here with us?' And they took offence at him. Then Jesus said to them, 'Prophets are not without honour, except in their own town, and

among their own kin, and in their own house.'
And he could do no deed of power there, except
that he laid his hands on a few sick people and
cured them. And he was amazed at their unbelief
(Mark 6.1–6).

There is room in me for Christ, the Christ who
is compassion, anger and gentleness, who is
infant, child, teenager and young adult, who is
craftsman, worker, story-teller, healer, host and
servant, who enables the finding of truth and the
puncturing of nonsense, who values touching and
companionship, who can be solitary and silent,
who knows what it is like to be treated as rubbish,
who carries the marks on his hands, who is Lord
of me, of my neighbour and of my enemy. There
is room for all this Christ of whom I know, and for
all the Christ whom I do not know. There is room
in me.

Christ is with us, our companion, but he will be at
our destination before us. The risen Christ tells the
disciples to go to Galilee, the place of confusion,
disorder and unbelief. They will find that he's there
ahead of them, and they will have to move swiftly
to keep up with him:

Then Jesus said to them, 'Do not be afraid; go and tell my brothers to go to Galilee; there they will see me (Matthew 28.10).

When we go out into the world, we do not take Christ with us. He is already there, as Lord and host in the scene into which we move. We go to recognize his presence, to help others to identify him.

Christ will be behind us when we leave. In my attempts to be a disciple, I will doubtless be as incompetent and clumsy as the original disciples. In his Gospel, St Mark is constantly reminding us how stupid and obstructive the trainee apostles were. At the end of the day, or at the end of the event, at the end of the year, or at the end of my life, I hand over what I have been trying to do. I trust that Christ will make something useful out of the mess. He will be behind me, picking up the pieces. He will secure all that is good from the past, so that I do not have to be anxious about its preservation.

Christ will be in front of me, leading me. He has promised that his Spirit will lead me into truth that I have not yet imagined and for which I have not been trained:

When the Spirit of truth comes, he will guide you into all truth; for he will not speak on his own, but will speak whatever he hears, and he will declare to you the things that are to come (John 16.13).

He will be in my relationships; like a link that joins two other links in a chain, he will come between me and the one who loves me, so that we do not dominate or control one another, but he will also bond us together so that we can rely on his security and not just on our emotions.

Christ is behind me; in his care I can leave, without anxiety, my parents, my ancestors, and all from whom I inherit the wealth of the earth. Christ is before me. The way of life that is being led by people of my generation in the Western world means that we are borrowing from our grandchildren; by the time they are my age, the earth may be damaged beyond repair and I dread to think how we may be blamed. But, in ways that I cannot imagine, I can still hope that, in Christ, nothing will be able to separate them from the love of God.

And Christ rules in all the other dimensions suggested in this verse.

This verse is the climax of the Breastplate. Like the rest of the hymn, it focuses, without apology, on **me**, my needs and my interests. But it is all the time directed at the Other, at Christ. We can use it as a basis for meditation or spiritual exercises. We can take it, phrase by phrase, and link it to our breathing, taking a deep breath, in and out, while reflecting on each phrase. Or we can take it a phrase each day, picking up the phrase and claiming it at odd moments as the day passes. Or we can take it as a base for intercession, replacing each 'me' with the name of the person we are praying for. We can substitute 'you' for 'me', and then this verse becomes an excellent blessing for a marriage, a welcoming for the newly born, a valediction for people on a journey, a commendation at a funeral, a dismissal at the end of worship.

All this is a million miles away from the kind of 'meditation' that is marketed as a consumer good, a self-regarding exercise that can be measured by one's contentment and adjustment and 'peace of mind'. Such meditation is offered as a thing-in-itself, a set of techniques for getting a pleasurable or relaxed feeling, not as a meeting with God. I remember, years ago, a gathering where people were sharing with one another their relaxation techniques for this kind of meditation, and Archbishop Michael Ramsey broke into it with a sharp question, 'Relaxed for what?' I had earlier been listening to a priest in the City of London, who conducted lunch-hour relaxation classes in his church; the effect, as I understood him, was that his clients were sent back into the afternoon reinvigorated, to be sharper manipulators and more ruthless predators than their competitors who had been enjoying big business lunches. Our engagement with God is not supposed to enable us to adjust better to a destructive and violent world. If Christ is truly with us and within us, we shall find that we begin to share his own maladjustment. He too lived in a world where the wealth created by the work of the poor was diverted to enrich the privileged, a world where religion was used as a method for labelling one's enemies and excluding the misfits, a world where peace was maintained by a military machine that crucified those whom it could identify as terrorists. Jesus offered peace, but not as the world gives, and that could mean 'not peace but a sword':

Do not think that I have come to bring peace to the earth; I have not come to bring peace, but a sword (Matthew 10.34).

Like the prophets before him, Jesus refused to adjust to the status quo. He called his followers into a community of resistance and non-co-operation, and that is the realistic meaning of his invitation to them to be carriers of the cross. Martin Luther King yearned for the establishing of 'an International Association for the Advancement of Creative Maladjustment'. The shorter name for this association would be the Church of Jesus Christ.

This verse is a direct prayer to Christ, but we do not initiate this prayer. Prayer is possible because God in Christ has made himself accessible; he has come close to us in our world. It is his initiative. We respond, and by so doing we insist that the reality of Christ, who is alongside the poorest of our sisters and brothers, is a stronger reality than the great powers and structures that cause people to be poor. We can defy our present experience, in the name of the truer realm that is coming. This is when we pray for ourselves. And when we replace the 'me' with the name of someone else, our intercession links that person with the divine alternatives. We are affirming that there is another authority in the world, and we are in business to work for its establishing. This is especially true when the other person for whom we pray is the enemy, and to use this verse as a prayer for the enemy is a move towards the conversion of both of us. The powers that divide humanity against itself have met their match, in the one who is Saviour of friend and stranger alike. God the Holy Spirit prays in us, claiming our voice even when we have no words:

> Likewise the Sprit helps us in our weakness; for we do not know how to pray as we ought, but that very Spirit intercedes with sighs too deep for words (Romans 8.26).

We become a voice that expresses God's own longing for the kingdom to be realized on earth as it is in heaven. We demand of God that the kingdom should come; we set God free to claim our energies for this to happen. This is not an evasion of the practical struggle. On the contrary, by our prayer, we insist on recognizing the full scale of the conflict that we are in. We recognize that it is indeed not just a political or economic conflict 'against flesh and blood', but a conflict with the spiritual realities that claim the allegiance of human structures and institutions.

So this is our response to the terrors that we have recognized in the previous two verses. So much in our world suggests that evil triumphs, but against the evidence we can insist, in the words of Desmond Tutu's credo:

Goodness is stronger than evil,
Love is stronger than hate:
Light is stronger than darkness,
Life is stronger than death.
Victory is ours, Victory is ours
through him who loved us.[1]

Note

1 Published in John Bell, *There is One Among Us – Shorter Songs for Worship* (Glasgow, Wild Goose Publications, 1998), p. 30.

I Bind unto Myself the Name

I bind unto myself the name,
The strong name of the Trinity;
By invocation of the same,
The Three in One and One in Three.
Of whom all nature hath creation;
Eternal Father, Spirit, Word:
Praise to the Lord of my salvation,
Salvation is of Christ the Lord.

Like many Celtic prayers, the Breastplate comes full circle to its conclusion, and the final verse reclaims the opening commitment. We have been reminded of God's initiatives in creation and incarnation; we have voiced our defiance of the systems of evil. We have claimed the companionship of Christ.

We return to the central affirmation, that the fundamental basis of our being is in the nature of God as Trinity.

In the course of the day, I can pick up this dedication in the name of the Trinity, as a resource to call me back to the truth about myself. For instance, I may at times feel afraid of losing my support from other people. I may fail to fulfil expectations; I may be unable to meet deadlines; I may be unsuccessful in achieving goals. Or I may find myself obliged in conscience to stand up for truth or peace or justice in a way that will cut me off from everyone I rely on for my security. I may be required to stand alone. Can I take the risk of isolation? The gospel of God as Trinity assures me that the principle of unity, of bondedness, is eternally guaranteed. God is eternal belonging. My binding to the Trinity gives me confidence that I will not be fundamentally isolated. The bondedness of the One-in-Three is a guarantee that bondedness is at the heart of the universe. So I can take the risk; I will still belong.

At another stage of the day, I may feel threatened by the sense that I am just part of a general human mass, without any distinctiveness or personal quality. I seem to be merely part of someone else's programme. How can I be sure that there is a real 'me'? Am I just a number, a mass-produced non-entity? I may be tempted to compensate for this by parading myself with some special achievement or eccentricity or minority identity. I may be attracted by a programme to emphasize my group's exclusiveness, to stress our superiority over other identities, to put other people down. The gospel of God as Trinity assures me that the principle of distinctiveness is eternally guaranteed. My binding to God as Trinity gives me confidence that I am still unique, and I do not need to resort to tricks and injustice to prove it. The diversity within the Three-in-One is a guarantee that distinctiveness is at the heart of the universe, and I do not have to prove myself more clever or holy than anyone else.

In the heart of God, separateness is overcome, and distinctiveness is vindicated.

Because the real 'I' is bonded to God as Trinity, the 'ego' that feels threatened can rest, and face the day without anxiety.

At the beginning of the day, I am born again to a new life. Each awakening is a little baptism; the Breastplate seals the baptism of the day, in the invocation of the Three-in-One and One-in-Three.

The Breastplate is a statement of faith and it is a song. It ends in praise. I not only affirm that these things are true, but I celebrate them, I give them supreme value. I worship. This is what I live by. The message echoes that even older song of holy defiance, the 'Te Deum'. Against all the divisive powers that set themselves up as rivals to the Creator; against the tinpot 'Hitlers' of ideology, race or religion; against the competitive acquisitiveness that grasps, grabs, deprives and destroys, we celebrate and insist:

You are God, we praise you;
you are the Lord and we acclaim you.

We sing this song in public, and we invite the power-bearers of the world to join us. We require them to acknowledge that they are not autonomous, that they are answerable to the Creator. That is the calling of the Church that praises, and it is our first contribution to the coming of the Kingdom.

Praise to the God of our salvation.

I bind unto myself today the strong name of the Trinity.

'St Patrick's Breastplate': translation from the original Irish

Several translations of the Breastplate have been made into English from the original Irish version. This one is by the celtic scholar, Kuno Meyer, in *Selections from Ancient Irish Poetry.*[1]

> I arise today
> Through a mighty strength, the invocation of
>   the Trinity
> Through belief in the Threeness
> Through confession of the Oneness
> Of the Creator of Creation.
>
> I arise today
> Through the strength of Christ's birth with his
>   baptism,

Through the strength of his crucifixion with his
    burial,
Through the strength of his resurrection with his
    ascension,
Through the strength of his coming down for
    judgement.

I arise today
Through the strength of the love of Cherubim,
In obedience of angels,
In the service of archangels,
In prayers of ancestors,
In predictions of prophets,
In preachings of apostles,
In faith of confessors,
In deeds of righteous men.

I arise today
Through the strength of heaven; –
Light of sun,
Radiance of moon,
Splendour of fire,
Speed of lightning,
Swiftness of wind,
Depth of sea,
Stability of earth,
Firmness of rock.

I arise today
Through God's strength to pilot me,
God's might to uphold me,
God's wisdom to guide me,
God's hand to guard me,
God's shield to protect me,
God's host to save me,
From snares of devils,
From temptations of vices,
From all who shall wish me ill,
Afar and near,
Alone and in multitude.

I summon today all these powers between
    me and those evils,
Against every cruel merciless power that
    may oppose my body and soul,
Against incantations of false prophets,
Against black laws of paganism,
Against spells of witches,
Against every knowledge that corrupts
    man's body and soul.

Christ to shield me this day,
So that there come to me abundance of
    reward.

Christ with me, Christ before me, Christ
    behind me,
Christ in me, Christ beneath me, Christ
    above me,
Christ when I lie down, Christ when I sit,
    Christ when I arise,
Christ in the heart of everyone who thinks
    of me,
Christ in the mouth of everyone who
    speaks of me,
Christ in every eye that sees me,
Christ in every ear that hears me.

Other versions conclude with a repeat of the opening:

I bind myself today,
To a strong power, an invocation of the
    Trinity,
I believe a Threeness with confession of a
    Oneness in the Creator of Judgement.

And then, a conclusion in Latin:

Salvation is the Lord's,
Salvation is the Lord's,

Salvation is Christ's,

Let your salvation, O Lord, Be ever with us.

Note

1 Kuno Meyer (trans.), *Selections from Ancient Irish Poetry* (London, Constable, 1913).